Sonny Chua's Cool Keys
10 irresistible piano solos
2

 For online audio backing tracks scan the QR code
or go to fabermusic.com/audio

FABER *ff* MUSIC

Contents

Going bananas! 4
Firestorm 6
Airy fairy 8
Midnight snack 10
Waltz it all about? No. 8 12
Hot and sassy 14
Angel 18
Feeling kooky 21
Ready to rumble 24
Around the world in 2 minutes… or less 27

Dedicated to our girls, Aria and Umi

© 2020 by Faber Music Ltd
First published in 2020 by Faber Music Ltd
Bloomsbury House
74–77 Great Russell Street
London WC1B 3DA
Music processed by Jackie Leigh
Audio recorded by Christopher Hussey
Cover design by Chloë Alexander
Printed in England by Caligraving Ltd
All rights reserved

ISBN10: 0-571-54184-4
EAN13: 978-0-571-54184-3

To buy Faber Music publications or to find out about the full range of titles available
please contact your local retailer or Faber Music sales enquiries:

Faber Music Limited, Burnt Mill, Elizabeth Way, Harlow, CM20 2HX, England
Tel: +44 (0) 1279 82 89 82
fabermusic.com

Celebrating Sonny Chua
(1967–2020)

Sonny Chua was an Australian composer, educator and pianist, known for his characterful and energetic musical style. His music delights in a spirited playfulness and he will undoubtedly be remembered by many for the sheer joy his compositions brought to their playing.

Born in Malaysia, Sonny lived in Kuala Lumpur, Singapore and Malacca before immigrating to Australia. He studied at the Melbourne Conservatorium of Music specialising in piano performance, but his heart was in composing piano music. Sonny composed numerous pieces for his own piano students, taking into account their interests, such as dinosaurs and fairies, but with a pedagogical focus to address various techniques. Sonny was a devoted advocate and spokesperson for music education, resulting in him becoming President of the Association of Music Educators (Victoria). This led to countless workshops, festivals and conferences all over the world, including presenting at the ISME World Conference in Malaysia and Brazil. His piano works are regularly heard at competitions for young musicians and have become standard repertoire in Australian examination syllabuses.

Sonny Chua's Cool Keys 1 and 2 explore a wealth of genres and styles and make for impressive performance pieces. Accompanied throughout by notes from the composer, both books also include audio of all the pieces to download. *Cool Keys 1* was recorded by Sonny himself, providing an invaluable insight into the energy that Sonny's playing exhibits.

We hope these collections of imaginative piano solos will be a fitting tribute to Sonny and inspire pianists of all ages to perform, for many years to come.

Going bananas!

Establish the anxiety of the piece by keeping the left-hand notes even and insistent!
Keep an eye on your fingering for transitioning between phrases.

Sonny Chua

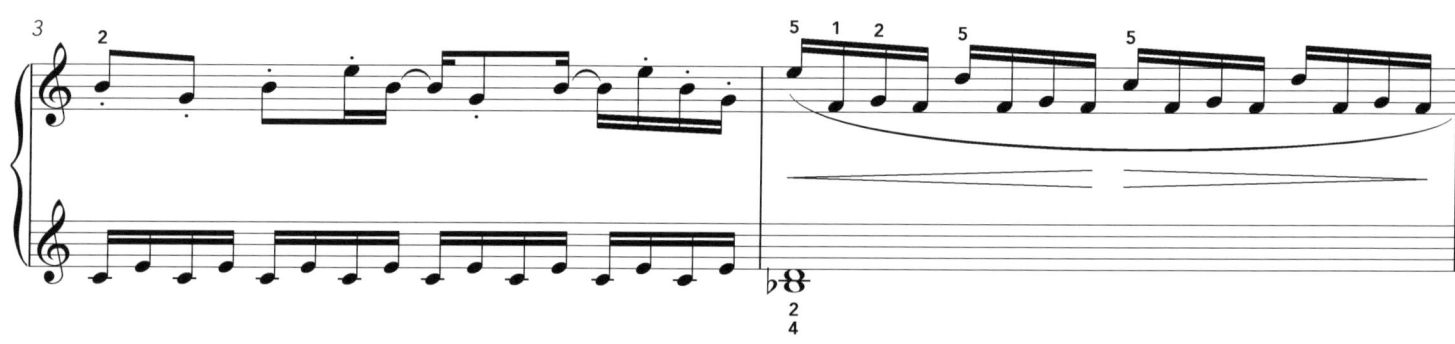

© 2020 Faber Music Ltd

Firestorm

Create the fury of flames with a steady pulse. Relish the raging bass
with lots of thunderous weight of the left arm.

Sonny Chua

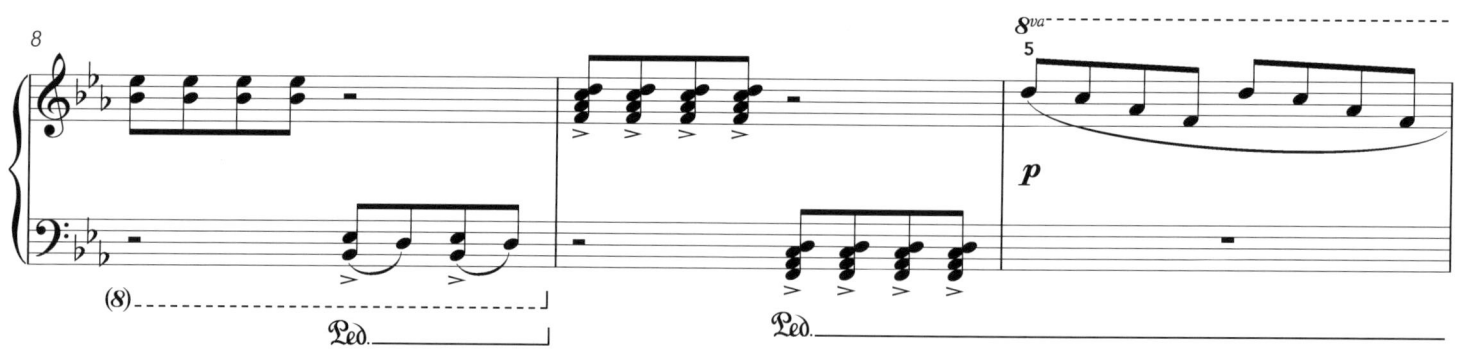

© 2020 Faber Music Ltd

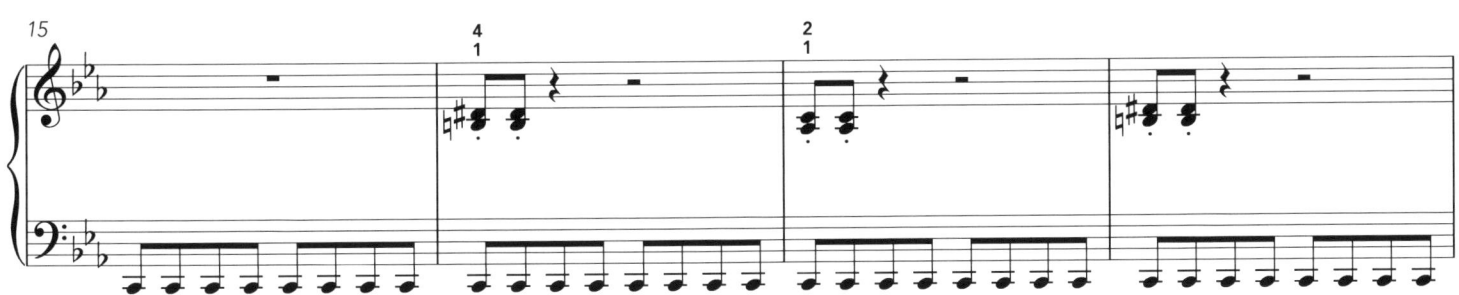

Airy fairy

Maintain the clarity of the notes with clean pedalling. Secret hint: hold down the first few notes of each bar as you lift the sustaining pedal and delay putting down the pedal to achieve this effect. Pedalling in this way is called 'finger pedalling'.

Sonny Chua

© 2020 Faber Music Ltd

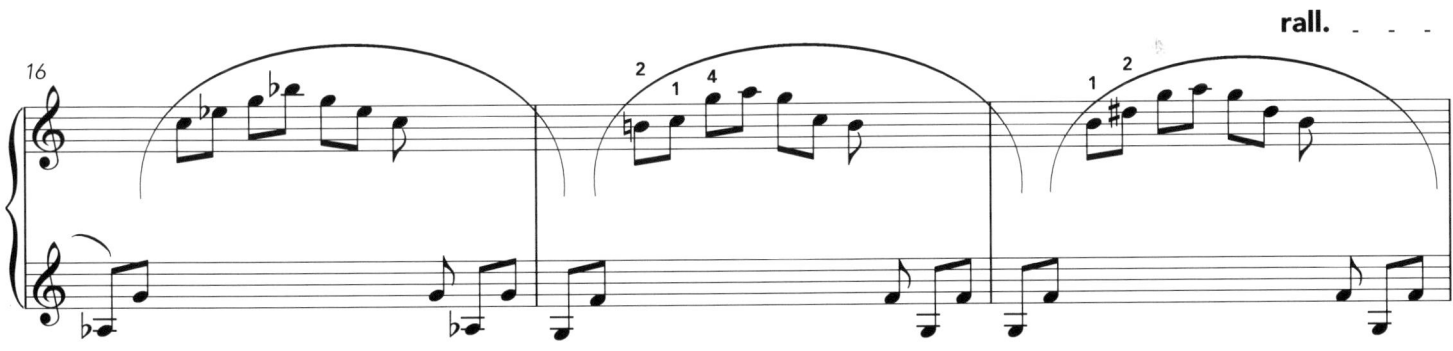

Midnight snack

Capture the sneakiness of the opening ostinato with light and short staccato notes, slyly contrasted with the slurred notes. Keep the accents ruthless and the urgency in the pulse steady.

Sonny Chua

Waltz it all about? No. 8

This is a piece of questions. Allow the end of each phrase to float gracefully and quizzically away.

Sonny Chua

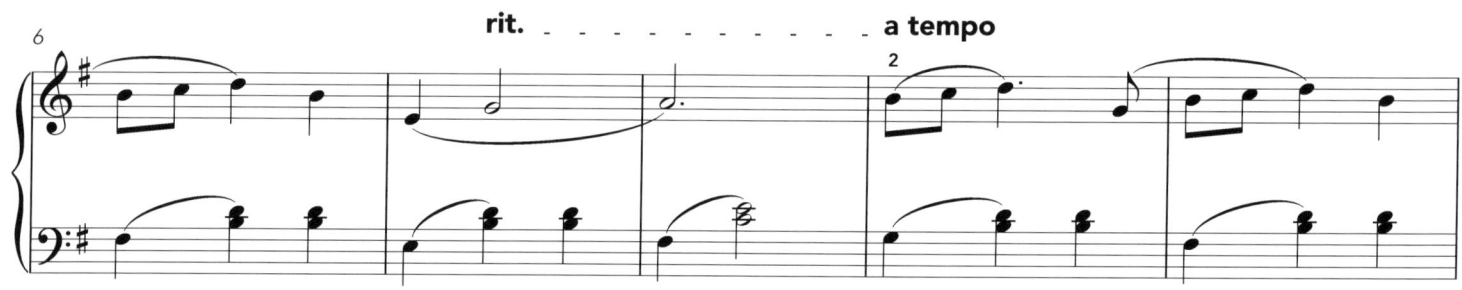
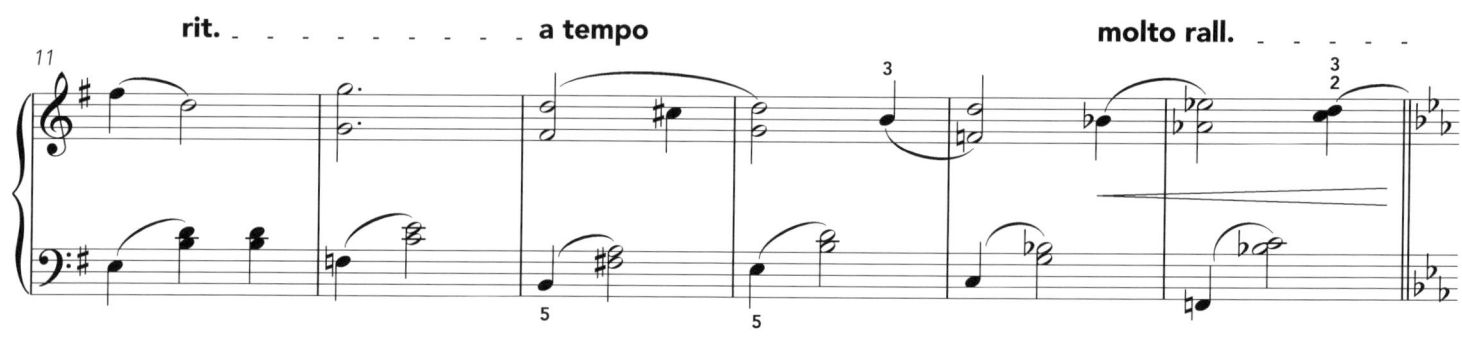

© 2020 Faber Music Ltd

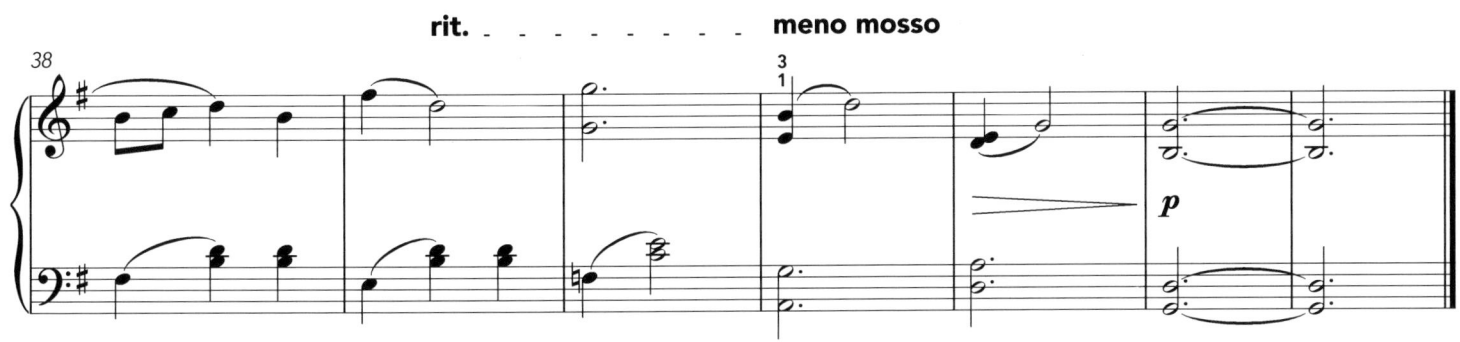

Hot and sassy

Let's rock 'n' roll! Keep the exuberance and vibrancy, playing with firm fingertips for precision and vigour. End the piece with *savoir faire*.

Sonny Chua

© 2020 Faber Music Ltd

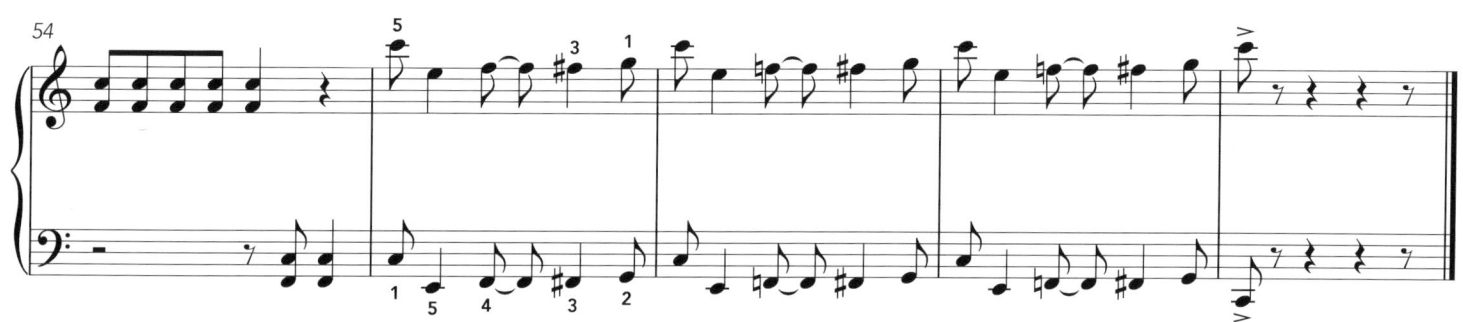

Angel

Capture the feeling of timelessness and eternal space. Let the bell's entrance reverberate below and above the swirling clouds in the left hand. Allow the surprising cheekiness of the second part of the piece to dance and spring with joy.

Sonny Chua

© 2020 Faber Music Ltd

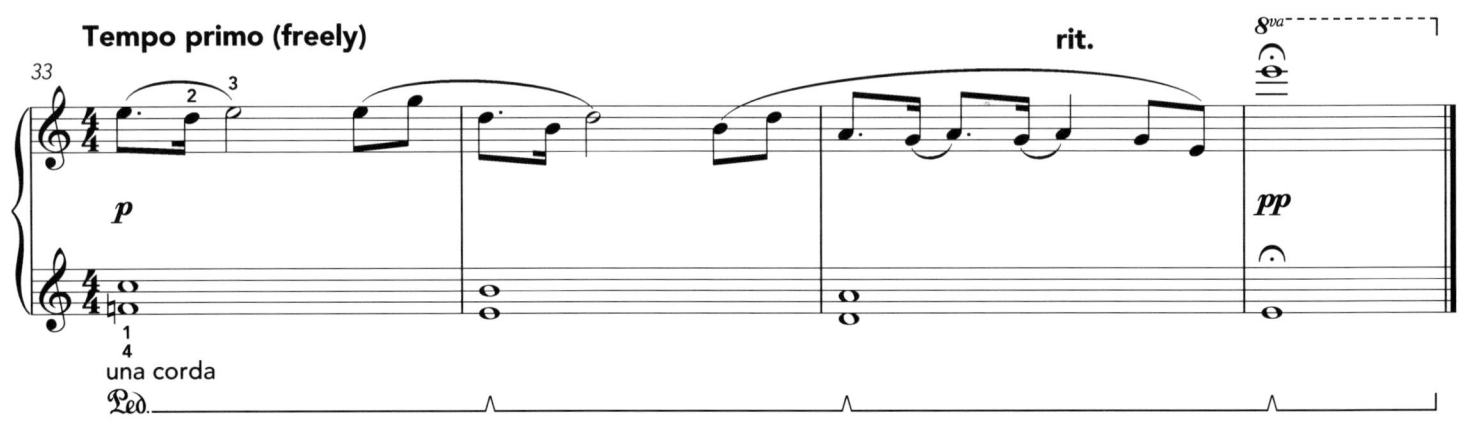

Feeling kooky

Relax into the groove and enjoy the funky rhythm! Keep a strong and steady pulse and be sure to choose fingerings that allow you to play comfortably.

Sonny Chua

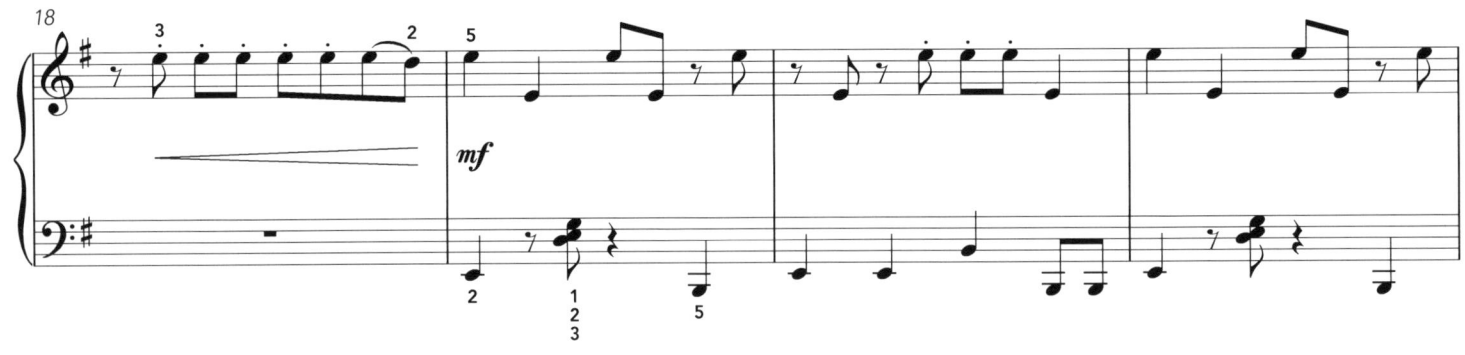
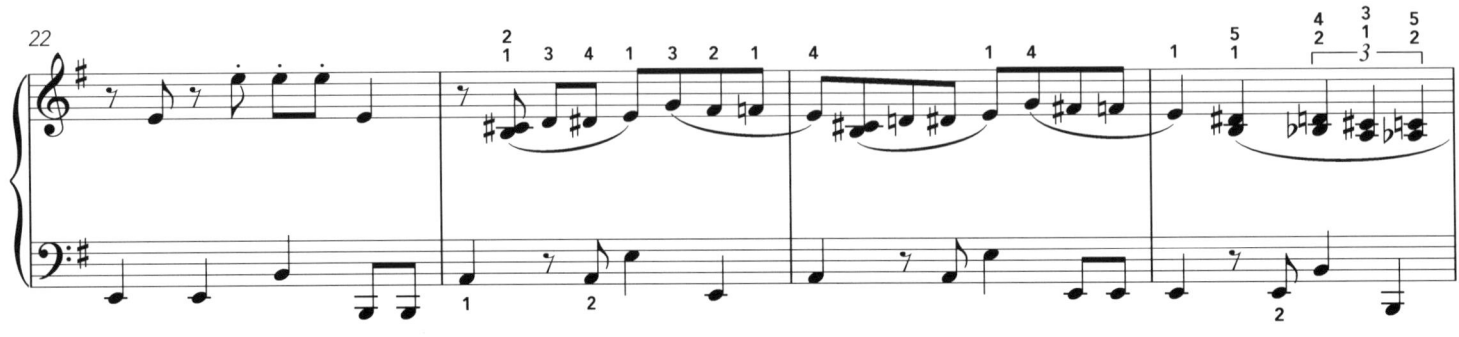
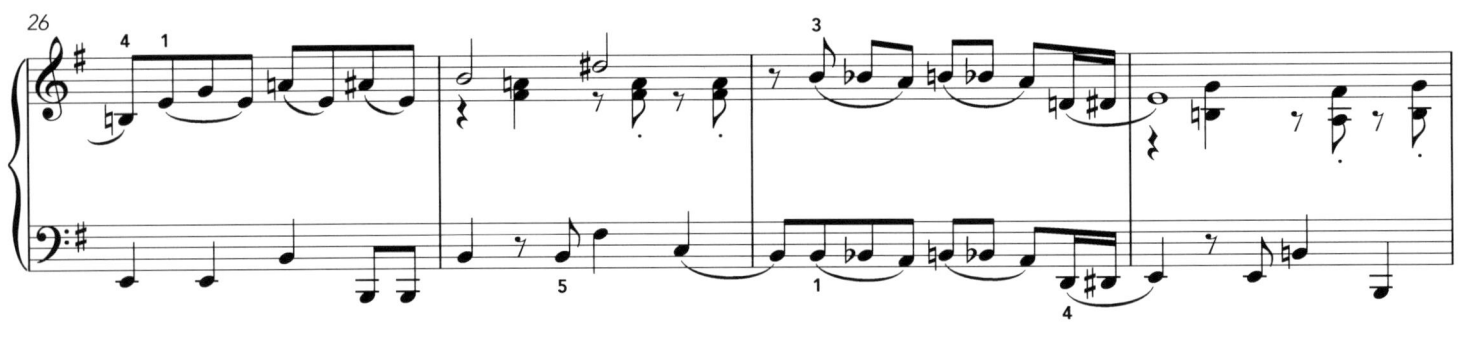
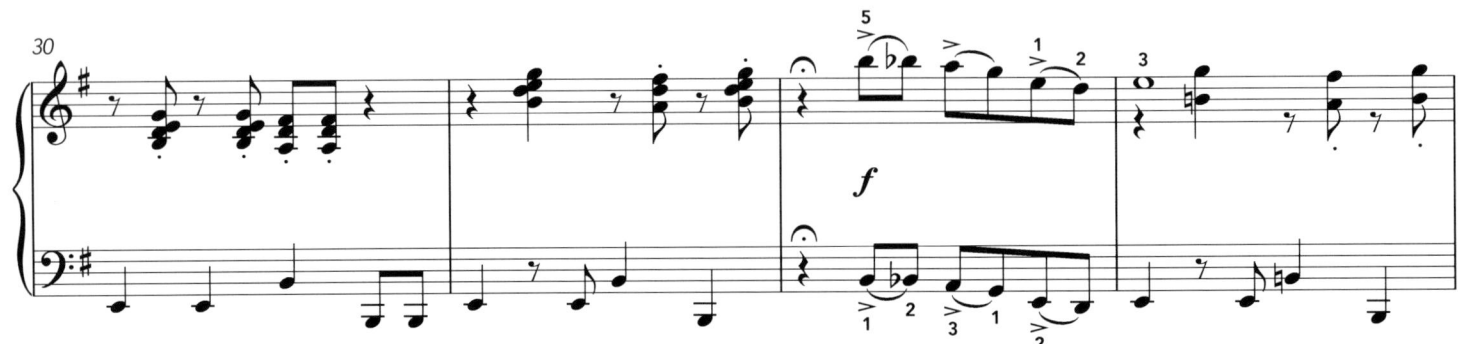

Ready to rumble

Sonny Chua

© 2020 Faber Music Ltd

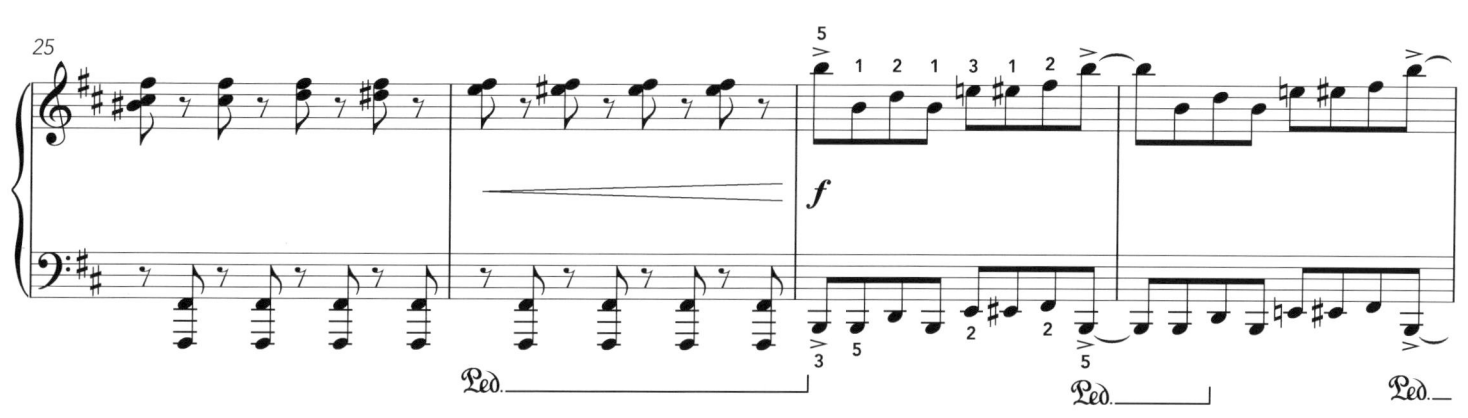

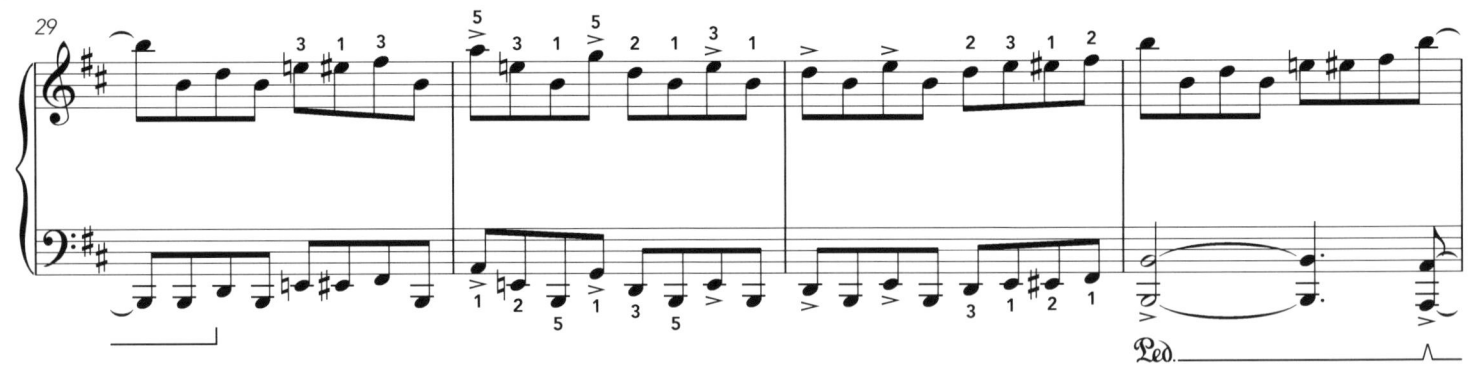

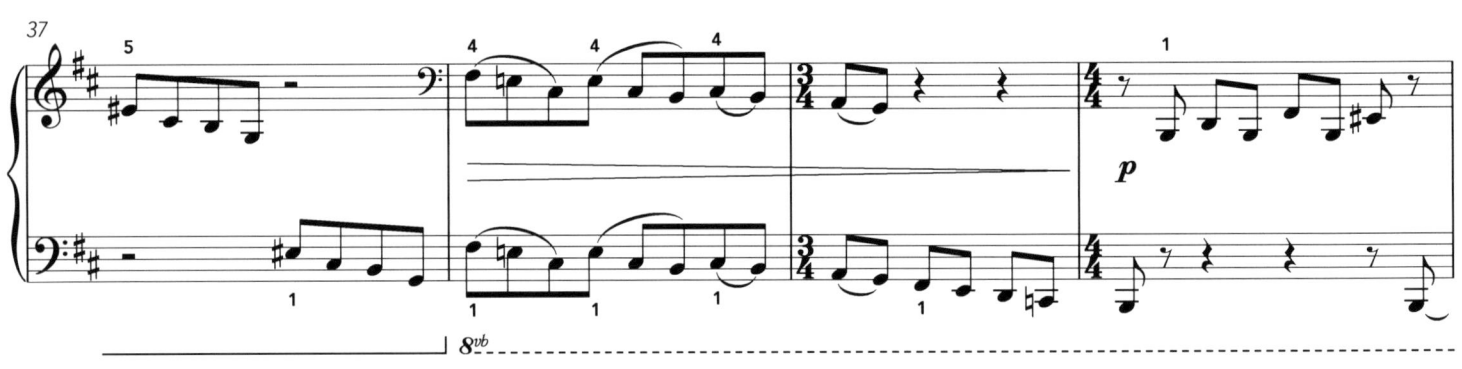

Around the world in 2 minutes... or less

Sonny Chua

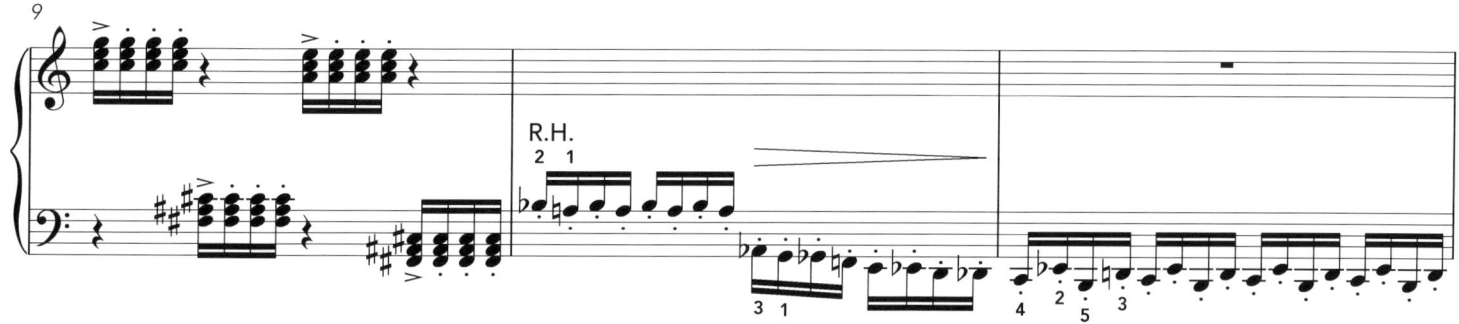

© 2020 Faber Music Ltd

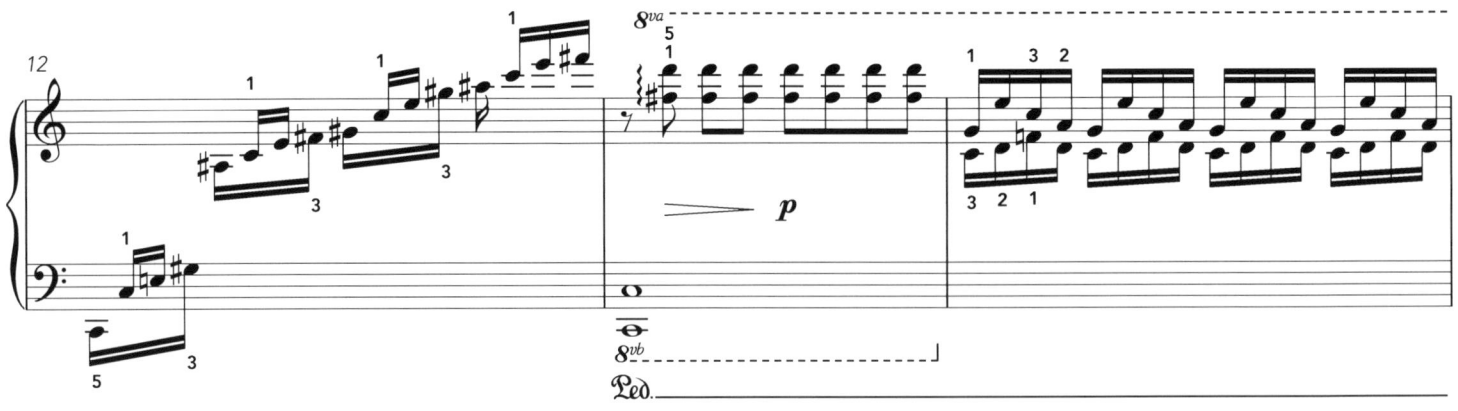
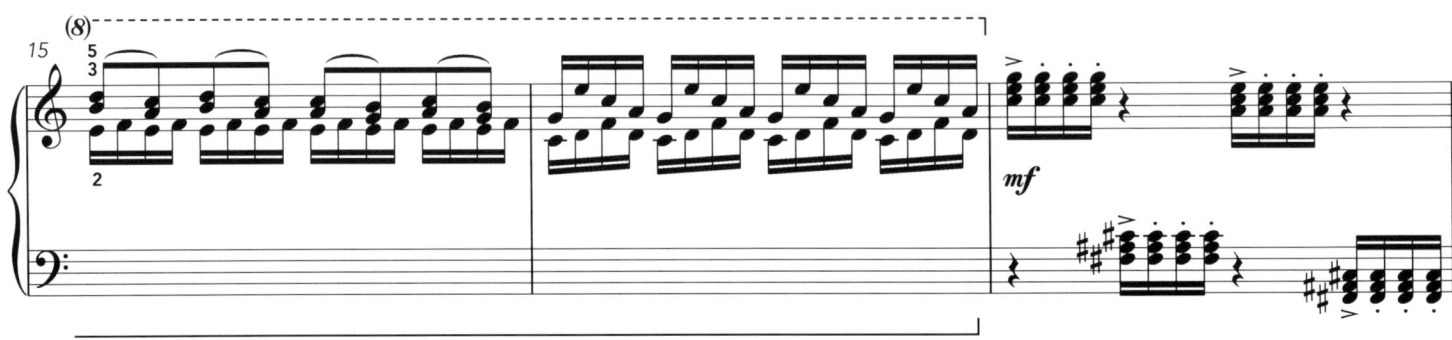
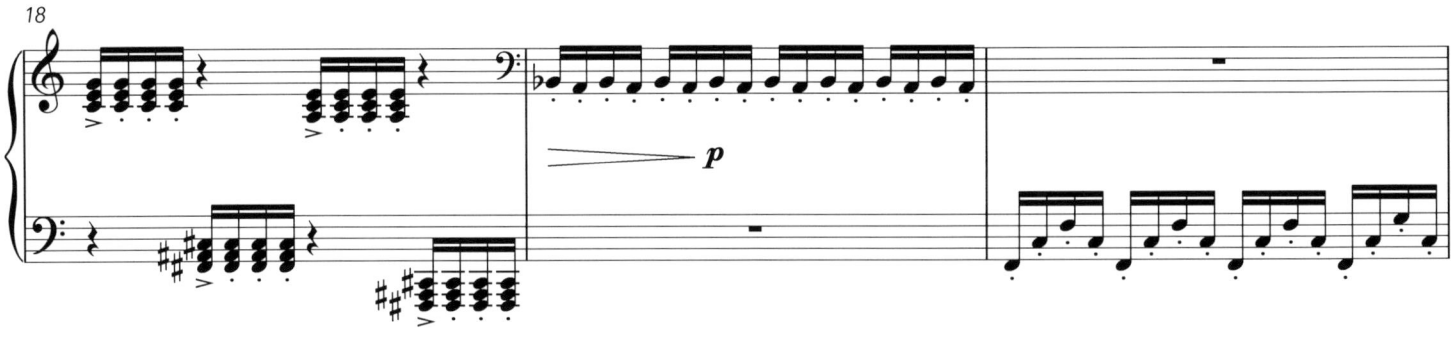
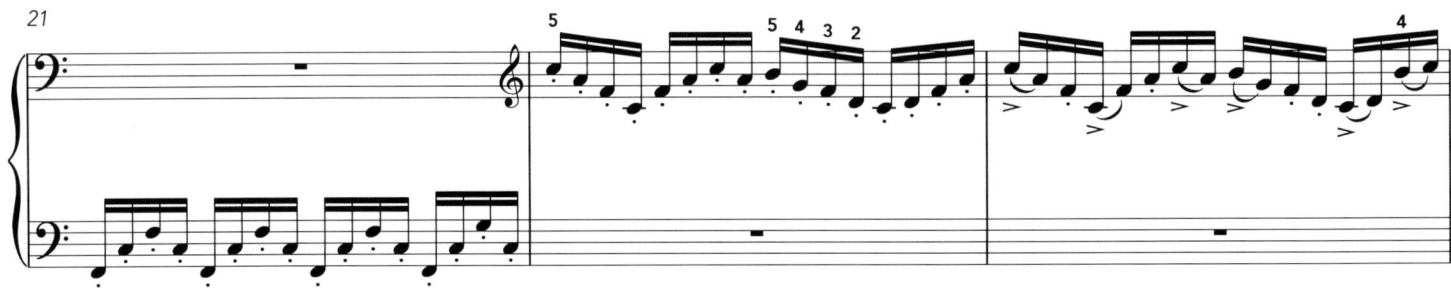

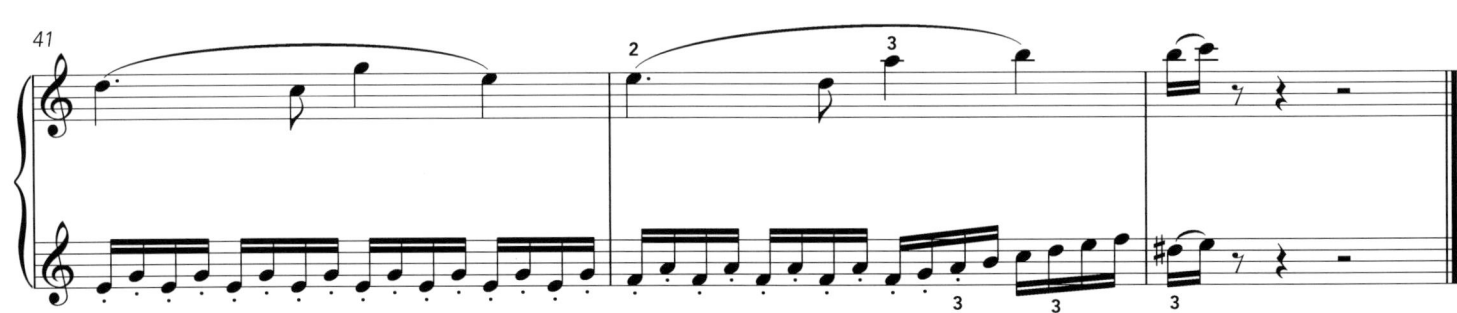